PRESS

FINDING THE BALANCE

AUTHOR
Lyman Coleman

PROJECT ENGINEER
Matthew Lockhart

CONTRIBUTORS
Jeff Coleman, Richard Guy

TYPESETTING
Sharon Penington

COVER DESIGN
Erika Tiepel

Photo on cover and repeated throughout book:
©1994, Elan Sun Star/Stock Imagery, Inc.

Scripture taken from
Today's English Version
Second Edition © 1992
Old Testament:
© American Bible Society 1976, 1992
New Testament :
© American Bible Society 1966, 1971, 1976, 1992
Published by
Thomas Nelson Publishers
Used by permission.

Seven Sessions on Lifestyle

Session		Bible Story	Team Building Goal
1	STRESS	The Storm/Luke 4:35-41	Team Sign Up
2	PARENTAL EXPECTATIONS	Mother's Request/Matthew 20:20-24	Learning to Share
3	PEER PRESSURE	Woman in Adultery/John 8:1-11	Going Deeper
4	MORAL ISSUES	John the Baptist Beheaded/Matthew 16	Affirmation
5	SEXUAL DESIRES	Uninvited Guest/Luke 7:36-50	Getting Personal
6	SPIRITUAL STRUGGLES	Paul's Conversion/Acts 9:1-19	Learning to Care
7	DECISIONS, DECISIONS	Banquet Excuses/Luke 14:15-24	Team Celebration

SERENDIPITY HOUSE / Box 1012 / Littleton, CO 80160 / TOLL FREE 1-800-525-9563

COACH'S BOX - BEHIND THE SCENES

"Serendipity is the facility of making happy, chance discoveries."

Horace Walpole, 1743

Horace Walpole, the great English storyteller, coined the word "serendipity" to describe what happened to three princes from the island of Sherri Lanka who experienced one surprise after another on a trip—totally unexpected. The "serendipity" in this program is the surprise that happens when you get together around a common cause and work together as a team to accomplish something . . . . together. Every session has a step-by-step process for team building, starting off with fun crowd breakers and communication games and ending up with shared prayer and caring. Here's a bird's eye view of the overall team-building design. Note how the "disclosure" level gradually flows from session to session.

GROUP AGENDA	PROGRESS REPORT
SESSION 1	
Team Sign Up.	**Check In Examination.**
Orientation. What's it all about.	Pinpoint where you are at the beginning
How it works. Make a commitment.	of this program - page 3.
SESSION 2	
Learning To Share.	**How's It Going?**
Tell us a little about yourself. Who are	What do you think about this program?
you? Where are you from?	On the disclosure scale - no risk.
SESSION 3	
Going Deeper.	**How Do You Feel About Your Team?**
Tell us more about yourself. Your values.	What's the trust level? On the
Your lifestyle. Why you do what you do?	disclosure scale - low risk.
SESSION 4	
Affirmation.	**Where Have You Improved?**
Let us tell you what we have observed about	Take the Progress Report on page 3 again.
you so far. What we appreciate about you.	On the disclosure scale - moderate risk.
SESSION 5	
Getting Personal.	**How Can We Help You in Prayer?**
Tell us about your concerns.	Learning how to pray. To be there
Struggles. Hopes. Dreams	for each other.
SESSION 6	
Learning To Care.	**How Can We Support You?**
Tell us what God is saying to you.	Learning how to minister to one
About your life. Your future.	another.
SESSION 7	
Team Celebration.	**What Happened To You?**
Evaluate your experience. Let us tell you	Take the Progress Report on page 3
the contribution you made to the team.	again to pinpoint your growth.

BEFORE. . .DURING. . .AFTER

Progress Report

Check to see where you are three times during this course. . . .at the end of the. . . .

- First session
- Fourth session
- Seventh session

If you had a complete physical, mental, relational and spiritual check up at the Mayo Clinic by doctors in these fields, what would they conclude about you. Record your pulse in each of these areas by putting a dot on the line below to indicate how you see yourself—1 being POOR and 10 being EXCELLENT health.

PHYSICALLY: I am feeling good physically. I stay in shape. Exercise regularly. Eat right. Sleep well. Enjoy life. Physically, I am. . .

Poor ————————————————————— Excellent
    1 2 3 4 5 6 7 8 9 10

MENTALLY: I am feeling good about myself. I build myself up. I have some God-given abilities. Strengths. I like who I am. Mentally, I am. . .

Poor ————————————————————— Excellent
    1 2 3 4 5 6 7 8 9 10

RELATIONALLY: I am feeling good about sharing myself with others. I make friends well. Deal with conflict. Reach out. Care. Forgive. Relationally, I am. . .

Poor ————————————————————— Excellent
    1 2 3 4 5 6 7 8 9 10

SPIRITUALLY: I am feeling good about my relationship with God. I am getting my spiritual life together, putting God first. Spiritually, I am. . .

Poor ————————————————————— Excellent
    1 2 3 4 5 6 7 8 9 10

Love the Lord your God with all your heart,
with all your soul. . .with all your mind,
and with all your strength. . .and
Love your neighbor as you love yourself.
Mark 12:30-31

SESSION 1 - COACH'S BOX

This course has two goals: (1) Spiritual formation/content, and (2) Spiritual experience/group building. Check this box at the beginning of each session for the group building plan for the session.

GAME PLAN: Team Sign Up. By the end of this session, the group will know what this course is all about and be ready to make a commitment for the next six sessions. . .to be on the team. The content for this session is "no risk" on the disclosure scale.

ON THE DISCLOSURE SCALE: Session 1.
No Risk___x_____High Risk

AGENDA/FORMAT: Four parts to the meeting. Chairs are rearranged for each step in the agenda.

STEP 1: Crowd Breaker	STEP 2: Warm Up	STEP 3: Bible Study	STEP 4: Caring
All together or Teams of 8 15 minutes	Groups of 2 15 minutes	Groups of 4 15-30 minutes	Teams of 8 15-20 minutes

TEAMWORK:
There is a method to the madness for these group sizes. Read the "Word to the Youth Leader" on page 46. First, make sure the entire youth group is committed to this program. In this session, the goal is to form into sub-teams of eight and agree to the guidelines. If your youth group is not more than ten or twelve, you may want to keep the whole group together. If you have more than twelve, we recommend sub-dividing into teams of six to eight—with an adult or older youth in each team. (*Again, reread the rationale on page 46*). In each session, follow the leader instructions in the margin. Trust us, there is method to the madness.

CROWD BREAKER/15 Minutes

Almost Anything Goes
    Have an Almost Anything Goes tournament, inviting other churches to participate as teams. Let's say you hold it at a farm. Some of the events to feature are the following:
    • A wheelbarrow obstacle course where the driver is blindfolded and the person sitting on the wheelbarrow gives directions.
    • A catapult made by jumping on a board, sending a playground ball into the air (the one hitting closest to a target wins).
    • A baking contest where in relay teams one person puts mud on a pie plate and tosses it to someone else who puts some "decorations" on top, then tosses it to someone else who stacks them (most pies made in a minute wins).
    • An obstacle course made with tires, boxes and things to jump over.
    • A balloon toss.

    Total team points determine the winner.*

*Reprinted by permission from Group Publishing.

4

LEADER:
Before you start, read A Word to the Youth Leaders, on page 46.

SESSION 1
Stress

WARM UP
Teams of 2
15 minutes

LEADER:
Pass out books. Explain teamwork principle. Explain diagrams on page 46 and theory behind 2's, 4's and 8's. Break into teams of 8's. Then, pair off in 2's for Warm Up. Read Intro-duction and call time after 15 minutes and move to Bible study.

A Do-It-Yourself Stress Test

Introduction. Welcome to the team. Your youth leader has probably explained what this program is all about. And the importance of teamwork in this program.

The program works like a sports training camp. In each session you will be put through a series of group building exercises, starting out with groups of 2, then groups of 4, and finally groups of 8.

The purpose of this program is to look at some of the things that cause pressure in your life—family expectations, peer pressure, moral decisions, sexual desires, spiritual struggles and uncertainty about the future.

In this session, you will have a chance to talk about your expectations for this program and the ground rules for being in the group. To get started, let's make our own stress test! Social scientists, Homes & Rahe, made up a stress test for adults where they assigned a point value for different life events. They found that if you got so many points, you were not only under heavy stress, you were likely to get sick! The only problem is, most of these events were only relevant for adults. Kids have stress too! Write in the spaces provided the point value your group would assign (from "1"—low to "100"—high) to the following, according to how much stress they cause. Then see what group members come up with when they score themselves.

EVENT	STRESS POINTS	EVENT	STRESS POINTS
Death of parent	___	Family conflicts	___
Death of sibling	___	Being broke	___
Divorce of parents	___	Arrested	___
Trying out for sports team	___	Breaking up	___
Parent out of work	___	Death of a friend	___
Harassed by drug-dealers	___	Changing schools	___
A victim of violence	___	Sexual pressure	___
Victim of school gossip	___	Failing a class	___
Starting a part-time job	___	Losing part-time job	___
Expected to make honor roll	___	Trying out for choir	___
		Your Total	___

LEADER:
Put two 2's together to
make 4's. Rearrange
chairs. Read Introduction
and scripture aloud. Save
30 minutes for last part—
Caring.

The Storms of Life

Introduction. The Bible study time in this program will be a little different from the usual Bible study. This is a program in personal growth and the Bible study time is mainly to let you talk about your own growth by taking a story of someone in the Bible and comparing your "story" to their "story". This might be called conversational Bible study.

In this session you will start with the story of Jesus and his disciples in a storm—a big storm—that caused a lot of stress.

There are two parts to the questionnaire: (1) **Looking Into The Story**—about the Bible story—and (2) **My Own Story**—about your own experience.

We recommend that you use groups of 4 to discuss the questionnaire—so that everyone can participate and you can finish in 30 minutes. Be sure to save the last 20 minutes at the close of this session to discuss your expectations and ground rules for the group.

Now, move into groups of four and listen to the Bible story. Then, follow the instructions for your discussion.

JESUS CALMS A STORM

[35]On the evening of that same day Jesus said to his disciples, "Let us go across to the other side of the lake." [36]So they left the crowd; the disciples got into the boat in which Jesus was already sitting, and they took him with them. Other boats were there too. [37]Suddenly a strong wind blew up, and the waves began to spill over into the boat, so that it was about to fill with water. [38]Jesus was in the back of the boat, sleeping with his head on a pillow. The disciples woke him up and said, "Teacher, don't you care that we are about to die?"

[39]Jesus stood up and commanded the wind, "Be quiet!" and he said to the waves, "Be still!" The wind died down, and there was a great calm. "Then Jesus said to his disciples, "Why are you frightened? Do you still have no faith?" [41]But they were terribly afraid and began to say to one another, "Who is this man? Even the wind and the waves obey him!"   Mark 4:35-41

Looking Into The Story: In groups of 4, let one person answer question #1, the next person answer question #2, etc. around the group. There are no right or wrong answers in the questionnaire, so feel free to express your opinion.

1. If you had been one of the disciples when the boat was about to sink, what would you have done?
   a. jumped overboard
   b. screamed for help
   c. started bailing water
   d. taken command
   e. acted like nothing was wrong

2. Why do you think the disciples awakened Jesus?
  a. they were afraid for his life
  b. they wanted all the help they could get
  c. they were afraid for their own lives
  d. they wanted Jesus to perform a miracle
  e. they were mad because he was sleeping

3. What was the tone in Jesus' voice when he said, "Why are you frightened?"
  a. scolding—"You guys are a bunch of wimps"
  b. disappointment—"Don't you know I am not going to let you down"
  c. compassion—"I know you are scared"
  d. resentment—"Why did you wake me up?"

4. Why did Jesus allow a storm to come up in the first place?
  a. he didn't; storms come up naturally
  b. he was asleep at the switch
  c. he wanted to test them
  d. he wanted to help them when they asked

My Own Story: Note the change in the way to share in this half of the questionnaire. Go around on question #1 and let everyone share their answer. Then, go around again on question #2. Be sure to save the last 20 minutes in this session for the last part—caring time.

1. What do you do when "storms" come up in your life?
  a. turn to someone I can trust
  b. turn to God
  c. stay pretty calm on the outside
  d. I have never gone through a "storm"
  e. withdraw into myself
  f. get very touchy and irritable
  g. play like nothing is wrong

2. If you told your parents about some of the struggles you are going through, what would they do?
  a. die on the spot
  b. kick me out of the house
  c. reach out to me
  d. give me all kinds of advice that I don't want
  e. share with me like an adult
  f. be very understanding

3. If you could compare your own life to the storm in the scripture, where are you right now?
  a. floating on smooth waters
  b. seeing just a few storm clouds
  c. sensing a storm is brewing
  d. the middle of the storm, bailing water like mad
  e. seeing the storm winds die down and calm return
  f. I never had to go through a "storm"

4. "Be Quiet! Be Still!" If Jesus were to speak these words to you today, what would they mean?
   a. settle down
   b. hang in there
   c. keep the faith, baby
   d. other:_____
   e. shut up and listen
   f. relax and let God handle this
   g. turn the controls of your life over to God

5. How do you feel about sharing your guts in this course?
   a. scared
   b. stupid
   c. no problem, these are my friends
   d. a little funny
   e. ok, but. . .
   f. I'm not the talking type
   g. other:_____

6. If you go into this program on personal growth with your youth group, what do you want to have understood at the beginning?
   a. anything that is shared in the group is kept in confidence
   b. I can say "I pass" anytime I want
   c. we are all in this together—no spectators in this game
   d. don't try to push religion on me
   e. we will respect each other
   f. this is not a Bible course—where you have to know all the right answers
   g. other:_____

CARING
Teams of 8
15-20 minutes

LEADER:
If you have more than ten to twelve, form groups of 8 by bringing two groups of 4 together. This group of 8 will stay together for the rest of this program—and meet together at the beginning and at the close of each session.

Team Sign Up

Introduction: Now is the time to decide what you want to get out of this course. For yourself. Your team. And to agree on the ground rules for team-work. Follow these four steps.

Step 1: Check in. Turn to page 3 and let everyone on your team explain where you are right now on these areas of your life. (You will have a chance to retake this test at the close of the course to see where you have changed).

Step 2: Expectations. Give everyone a chance to share the top two things you would like to get out of this course, using the list below:

____ to have fun
____ to talk about the real stuff in my life
____ to get to know the Bible
____ to get closer as a youth group
____ to go out and do something
____ to reach out to other kids at school
____ to grow in my faith
____ hanging out with my friends
____ other:_____

Step 3: Ground Rules. What are one or two things on the list below that you would like to include in the ground rules for being in this course? See if you can agree on these.

_____ ATTENDANCE: I will be at the meetings for the six sessions except in case of emergency.

_____ CONFIDENTIALITY: I will keep anything that is said at the meetings in confidence.

_____ PRAYER: I will pray for the others on this team.

_____ REACH OUT: I will invite others from school and church to join our group.

_____ MISSION PROJECT: I would like to see our team commit to a mission project at the close of this course.

_____ PARTY: I would like to see us celebrate this course together at the close with a party or retreat.

_____ ACCOUNTABILITY: I would like to see us report in each week on our spiritual walk with Christ.

Step 4: Prayer Partner. Inside of your team, choose one or two others to conclude this meeting. . .and every meeting for the next six sessions. . .with a time of prayer. Before you pray, "report" on how you are feeling. . .and where you want your prayer partner to pray for you this week. THEN, CALL DURING THE WEEK TO ASK "HOW'S IT GOING?"

LEADER:
At the close of this session, bring all of the teams together to reinforce the commitment—to be present every session.

SESSION 2 - COACH'S BOX

GAME PLAN: Learning to Share. By the end of this session, the group will be underway and ready for a progress report. How's It Going? Tell us what you think about the program. The content for this session is "low risk" on the disclosure scale.

ON THE DISCLOSURE SCALE: Session 2
No Risk_____x_____High Risk

AGENDA/FORMAT: Four parts to the meeting. Chairs are rearranged for each step in the agenda.

STEP 1: **Crowd Breaker** All together or Teams of 8 15 minutes	STEP 2: **Warm Up** Groups of 2 15 minutes	STEP 3: **Bible Study** Groups of 4 15-30 minutes	STEP 4: **Caring** Teams of 8 15-20 minutes

TEAMWORK:
There is a method to the madness for these group sizes. Read the "Word to the Youth Leader" on page 46. Make sure the entire youth group is committed to this program. In this session, the goal is to build upon the team concept layed out in Session 1. If your youth group is not more than ten or twelve, you may want to keep the whole group together. If you have more than twelve, we recommend sub-dividing into teams of six to eight—with an adult or older youth in each sub-team. Follow the instructions in the margin.

CROWD BREAKER/15 Minutes

Project-a-Skit
This is a modern version of the old shadow game.

Use an overhead projector as a light source to silhouette your image onto a white sheet suspended between your audience and the actors. Any item or drawing that is put on the viewing glass of the projector will accompany the shadows cast by the performers.

Here's a sample of the wild effects you can produce. Stand two people, one behind the other, so that they cast a single shadow on the sheet. Now place a small knife blade on the projector and move it in a sawing motion from the top to the bottom of the people shadow. When completed, have the two actors fall to opposite sides to end this dramatic visual.

Experiment with the projector using images such as two hands closing together, a shoe, pencils, paper cutout monsters, or wherever your imagination leads.

Divide into teams and create fun mini-dramas. Award a prize to the best presentation.

Use Project-a-Skit to liven up special events such as Halloween parties, Christmas get-togethers and Easter breakfasts.

Be prepared for shadow marathons. Some people can't quit!*

*Reprinted by permission from Group Publishing.

SESSION 2
Expectations

. **LEADER:**
Recap the last session.
Repeat the teamwork
principles. Ask teams of 8
to divide into 2's—not the
same person as last session.

How I See Myself

Introduction. In the last session, you talked about your expectations for this program and set the ground rules for your youth group for this program. Now, you are ready to start on the process of building your youth group into a support group—where you can talk about the deeper issues in your life.

This session has two objectives: (1) to let you talk about parental expectations—and how they contribute to pressure in your life, and (2) to let you tell a little more about yourself to your team—the small group that you will be a part of for the six remaining sessions in this program. To get started, get together with one other person from your team (not the same person that you were with in the last session) and discuss the exercise below.

Finish the sentence: "I see myself more like a _____ than a _____" by choosing one of the two options under #1. Then, let your partner do the same on #1. Then, go to #2 and both of you finish the sentence, etc. . . until you have worked through all of the allegories.

Now, move into groups of 2 and use this exercise to explain to your partner how you see yourself.

I SEE MYSELF MORE LIKE A _____ THAN A _____.

1. quiet lake..rushing stream
2. cultured pearl ....diamond in the rough
3. glossy photo ....original painting
4. short story...heavy novel
5. country road..super highway
6. 100 yard dash ....cross country run
7. Cadillac...Model T Ford
8. clinging vine ....touch me not
9. morning ....evening
10. library...comic book

FEEDBACK: (For your partner to finish about you)

1. Of all of the people that make up a circus team, I think you would make a good. . . .

2. Of all of the comic strip characters or movie stars, you remind me of. . .

11

A Pushy Parent

Introduction. You may think your parents don't care about you sometimes. But what if your parent went to Jesus and asked him to make you his prime minister?

In the Bible story, you will have a chance to see what happened in this situation, and to talk about some of your own "stories." The questionnaire below has two parts: (1) **Looking Into The Story** and (2) **My Own Story.**

Listen to the story as it unfolds in the Scripture. Then, move into groups of four and discuss the questionnaire: (1) **Looking Into The story**—about the Bible story, and (2) **My Own Story**—about your own experience.

The questionnaire has multiple-choice options and there are no right or wrong answers—so feel free to express your opinions.

Be sure to save the last 20 minutes at the close of this session for the Caring time.

Now, listen to the Bible story. Then, move into groups of four to share your responses.

A MOTHER'S REQUEST

²⁰Then the wife of Zebedee came to Jesus with her two sons, [James and John] bowed before him, and asked him for a favor.
²¹"What do you want?" Jesus asked her.
She answered, "Promise me that these two sons of mine will sit at your right and your left when you are King."
²²"You don't know what you are asking for," Jesus answered the sons. "Can you drink the cup of suffering that I am about to drink?"
"We can," they answered.
²³"You will indeed drink from my cup," Jesus told them, "but I do not have the right to choose who will sit at my right and my left. These places belong to those for whom my Father has prepared them."
²⁴When the other ten disciples heard about this, they became angry with the two brothers.   Matthew 20:20-24

Looking Into The Story: In groups of 4, let one person answer question #1, the next person question #2, etc. through the four questions.

1. Who are you embarrassed for in this story?
   a. Jesus
   b. the mother of the two sons
   c. the two sons

2. Why do you think the mother did this?
   a. her two sons put her up to it
   b. she was just acting like a mother
   c. she honestly wanted the best for her sons
   d. she didn't realize what she was asking

3. When Jesus told the mother, "You don't know what you are asking," what was he really saying?
   a. ma'am, you're embarrassing your sons
   b. you've got to be kidding
   c. your sons don't deserve that honor
   d. sorry—it's not my decision to make

4. How do you think the two sons are feeling after all of this?
   a. humiliated—like crawling into a hole
   b. mad at their mother
   c. hoping the ten other disciples will not hold it against them
   d. disappointed in Jesus

My Own Story: Note the change in the way to discuss the questions. Go around your group on the first question and let everyone answer. Then, go around again on the next question etc.

1. What is the closest your mother (or father) came to embarrassing you in public?
   a. insisting that you "perform" for the relatives
   b. showing your baby pictures to your girlfriend/boyfriend
   c. coming to a school event and clapping or cheering too loudly
   d. telling a secret family story to your high school friends
   e. crying in public

2. Which of the following comes closest to the truth concerning your parent(s) expectations for you?
   a. my parents expect very little—I wonder if they even care
   b. my parents expect too much—I can never live up to their expectations
   c. my parent's expectations are high enough to challenge me, but not too high to discourage me
   d. my parents have helped me to set my own expectations

3. Are you living up to your parent's expectations?
   a. are you kidding
   b. I'm trying
   c. yes
   d. I think I am above their expectations for me

4. When you have a difference with a parent over expectations, what have you found helpful?
   a. tell them to stay out of my life
   b. take this opportunity to sit down and talk
   c. tell them what they want to hear and forget it
   d. try to see where they are coming from
   e. agree together on the expectations
   f. put it in writing

5. What issues cause the greatest conflict between you and your parent(s)? (top three)

___ chores	___ discipline
___ grades	___ drugs/alcohol
___ curfew	___ manners
___ going to church	___ language
___ clothes	___ respect
___ hair	___ relatives
___ allowance	___ Twinkies in the fridge
___ TV	___ your future
___ keeping room clean	___ car
___ music	___ money
___ friends	___ sex
___ boyfriend/girlfriend	___ telephone
___ favoritism	___ lack of consistency

6. Of the three issues you identified in the last question, who do you think causes the problem? For each issue, put one of these symbols:

M = Me (It's my problem or I cause the problem)

P = Parent (It's their problem or they cause the problem)

O = Other (someone or something else is the cause of the problem)

7. When you get to be a parent, what are you going to do differently?
a. I am going to let my kids set their own rules
b. I am going to sit down with my kids and explain things
c. I am going to spend more time with my kids
d. I probably will do about the same

CARING
Teams of 8
15-20 minutes

LEADER:
Bring teams back together for Step 1 and 2. Then, Step 3 with prayer partners for this course.

Team Check-In: How's It Going?

Introduction: After two sessions in this program, stop the camera and evaluate what you think about the program. . .and what you would like to change.

Regather with your team and go over the questions together. Be sure to save the last few minutes to be with your prayer partner (Step 3).

Step 1: Check Your Pulse. What do you appreciate most about this course? Go around and let everyone share one or two things.

___ fun times
___ studying the Bible
___ close relationships
___ feeling like I belong
___ sharing our problems
___ praying for each other
___ reaching out to others
___ other:_____

Step 2: I Wish. If you could have one wish for this program, what would be your wish? Finish the sentence, I wish we could have. . .

___ more sharing about each other
___ more time for Bible Study
___ more fun
___ more reach out
___ more trips
___ less joking around
___ less gossip
___ less study
___ other:_____

Step 3: Prayer Partner. Get together with your prayer partner that you started with last week, and describe the last seven days in your life as a weather report. Then, close in prayer for each other. Finish the sentence, "This past week has been. . ."

❑ Blue sky, bright sunshine all week long—NO PROBLEMS
❑ Partly cloudy most of the week—A FEW PROBLEMS AT HOME
❑ Severe storms all week long
❑ mixed—some days sunny, some days cloudy
❑ warming trend—getting better
❑ tornado/hurricane—DISASTERS!
❑ other:_____

SESSION 3 - COACH'S BOX

GAME PLAN: Going Deeper. At the end of this session, the group will be asked to express how they feel about their group—whether they are "playing as a team" or "just looking on." On the disclosure scale, this session will be medium to low risk.

ON THE DISCLOSURE SCALE: Session 3
No Risk_____x_____High Risk

AGENDA/FORMAT: Four parts to the meeting. Chairs are rearranged for each step in the agenda.

STEP 1: **Crowd Breaker** All together or Teams of 8 15 minutes	STEP 2: **Warm Up** Groups of 8 15 minutes	STEP 3: **Bible Study** Groups of 4 15-30 minutes	STEP 4: **Caring** Teams of 8 15-20 minutes

CROWD BREAKERS/15 Minutes
Improvisation

Here's a fun crowd breaker. Give each group member two slips of paper. On one, have each person write his or her name. On the other, have each person write a situation to act out.

Put the papers with names on them in one can, and the papers with the situations in another. Draw a slip of paper from the situation can. See how many people the situation requires, then draw that many slips from the container with names in it. Those people act out what's on the paper.

Here are some examples of situations:
• Lucy tries to persuade Charlie Brown to kick a football while she holds it.
• Adam, Eve and the serpent in the Garden of Eden.
• All the youth group members find themselves thrust into the future or the past.*

Knee Sit

Here's a good crowd breaker—and a good exercise in group unity.

Everyone gets in a circle and turns to the left, facing the back of the next person. Then, on the count of three, everyone sits down on the knees of the person behind him or her, still holding to the hips of the person ahead of him or her.

If everyone sits in unison and no one falls off, you should be able to stay in that position for some time, quite comfortably.

Vary the game by having people stay in the sitting position and walk forward, walk backward, or walk to the beat of a favorite song.*

*Reprinted by permission from Group Publishing.

SESSION 3
Peer Pressure

Who Influences You?

Introduction. In this session, you are going to deal with the issue of peer pressure—how your friends influence you.

To get started, get together with one person from your team (not the same person as last week) and discuss who influences you most in making decisions about things in your life. In each category, check two columns—either (1) parents, (2) brother/sister, (3) friends, (4) teachers, (5) church/youth group or (6) TV/radio.

Who influences	my parents	my brother/sister	my friends	my teachers	my church or youth group	TV/radio
How I spend my time						
What I feed my mind						
What I look at						
Where I take a stand						
Where I draw the line						
What I believe						
What I want out of life						
How I see myself						
How I handle fear, failure, guilt						

17

Pressured by the Crowd

Introduction. The story of the woman caught in the act of adultery is a good example of peer pressure. The Pharisees put a lot of pressure on Jesus to go along with the crowd and condemn this girl.

Listen to the story carefully. Try to put yourself in the shoes of Jesus. See how he dealt with the dilemma that he faced. Then, get together in groups of four and discuss the questionnaire. There are no right or wrong answers to the questions, so feel free to express your opinion.

Be sure to save the last 20 minutes at the close of this session to get together with your team to wrap up the session.

Now, move into groups of four and listen to the Bible story.

THE WOMAN CAUGHT IN ADULTERY

¹Then everyone went home, but Jesus went to the Mount of Olives. Early the next morning he went back to the temple. The whole crowd gathered around him, and he sat down and began to teach them. The teachers of the Law and the Pharisees brought in a woman who had been caught committing adultery, and made her stand before them all. "Teacher," they said to Jesus, "this woman was caught in the very act of committing adultery. In our Law Moses gave a commandment that such a woman must be stoned to death. Now, what do you say?" They said this to trap him, so they could accuse him. But Jesus bent over and wrote on the ground with his finger. As they stood there asking him questions, he straightened up and said to them, "Whichever one of you has committed no sin may throw the first stone at her." Then he bent over again and wrote on the ground. When they heard this they all left, one by one, the older ones first. Jesus was left alone, with the woman still standing there. He straightened up and said to her, "Where are they, woman? Is there no one left to condemn you?"

"No one, sir," she answered.

"Well, then," Jesus said, "I do not condemn you either. Go, but do not sin again."   John 8:1-11

Looking Into The Story: In groups of 4, let one person answer question #1, the next person question #2, etc., as there are no right or wrong answers.

1. If you had been Jesus when the woman caught in the act of adultery was brought before him, how would you have felt?
   a. embarrassed
   b. intimidated by the Pharisees
   c. angry at the Pharisees
   d. mad for being put on the spot
   e. ashamed for the woman
   f. concerned for the woman
   g. torn between mixed feelings

2. Why do you think Jesus bent over and wrote on the ground?
a. to collect his thoughts
b. to take the attention away from the woman
c. to write something for the Pharisees to see—such as their sins
d. to keep from getting so angry that he lost it
e. other:_____

3. If you had been in this situation, what would be your biggest pressure?
a. to go along with the crowd—peer pressure
b. to do what the law required—legal pressure
c. to please the Pharisees—to be politically correct
d. to compromise your own convictions on adultery
e. to be compassionate and forgiving at the same time
f. to deal with your own moral failure

4. How did Jesus deal with the pressure?
a. he refused to make a decision
b. he refused to go along with the crowd
c. he stated his position and made others make a decision
d. he did what he thought was right
e. he compromised what he thought was right because of what he thought was loving

5. Why did the crowd slip away when Jesus said: "Whichever one of you has committed no sin may throw the first stone at her"?
a. because they had all committed adultery
b. because nobody wanted to claim they were perfect
c. because Jesus made the people stop and think—one by one—by asking one person to step forward
d. because crowds are that way—they are a bunch of cowards

My Own Story: Note the shift in sharing procedure. Go around on question #1 and let everyone answer the question. Then, go around again on question #2, etc.

1. When it comes to going against the crowd, who are the hardest people for you to stand up against?
a. teachers/authority figures
b. teammates/sports figures
c. friends at school
d. friends at church
e. boyfriend/girlfriend
f. other:_____

2. How tough is it to face the following pressures from the crowd? Rate yourself from 1 to 10—1 being EASY and 10 being HARD—in each category. Then, share with the group your easiest and your hardest.

Doing drugs and getting wasted
EASY   1   2   3   4   5   6   7   8   9   10   HARD

Letting others cheat off of you
EASY   1   2   3   4   5   6   7   8   9   10   HARD

Lying to your parents to cover for your friends
EASY   1   2   3   4   5   6   7   8   9   10   HARD

Sticking to your moral convictions
EASY   1   2   3   4   5   6   7   8   9   10   HARD

Sex (when your friends are sexually active)
EASY   1   2   3   4   5   6   7   8   9   10   HARD

Cursing/Profanity
EASY   1   2   3   4   5   6   7   8   9   10   HARD

Dirty jokes/Pornography/X-rated movies
EASY   1   2   3   4   5   6   7   8   9   10   HARD

Stealing
EASY   1   2   3   4   5   6   7   8   9   10   HARD

3. What have you found helpful in dealing with peer pressure?
   a. stay away from the wrong crowd
   b. bring your friends home where they can get to know your parents
   c. let your friends know where you stand on issues and why
   d. bring your friends to youth group where you talk about stuff openly
   e. make sure you have a better idea for every party
   f. go to a Christian school
   g. just say no

4. If you had to give your youth group a grade on how well you support each
   other and stand together against peer pressure, what would the grade be?
   a. I would give our youth group an A+
   b. I'd give us a B+ for effort
   c. well, I'd give us a C-
   d. sorry you asked

5. If the woman who was caught in adultery came to your youth group, how
   would she feel?
   a. weird
   b. uncomfortable at first
   c. she would feel right at home
   d. I hope she would feel accepted

How Do You Feel About Your Team?

Introduction: You have been together for three sessions. Take your pulse on how you feel about your group. Steps 1 and 2 are for your team together. Step 3 is with your prayer partner.

Step 1: Report In. If you could compare your involvement in this program to somewhere on the diagram below, where would you be:

- In the grandstand—for spectators—just looking on
- On the bench—on the team—but not playing
- On the playing field—where the action is
- In the showers—on the injury list

GRANDSTAND
(For spectators)

BENCH (team)

PLAYING FIELD
(Where the action is)

THE SHOWERS

Step 2: Teamwork. How would you describe the way you work together as a team in sports language? Finish the sentence: When we play together we're. . .

- jittery—like in our first game
- learning to trust each person on the team
- awkward—but we're improving
- fourth and goal to go—let's get it done!

Step 3: Prayer Partner. Get together with your prayer partner for this program and check to see how it went last week. Then, spend a little time in prayer for each other. Start off by picking a number from 1 to 10—1 being TERRIBLE and 10 being GREAT—to describe how last week went.

SESSION 4 - COACH'S BOX

GAME PLAN: Affirmation. At the end of this session, the group will do two things: (1) Retake the Progress Report on page 3 and (2) Affirm each other for the contribution each person is making to the team. On the disclosure scale, this session will be medium risk.

ON THE DISCLOSURE SCALE: Session 4.
No Risk_____x_____High Risk

AGENDA/FORMAT: Four parts to the meeting. Chairs are rearranged for each step in the agenda.

STEP 1: **Crowd Breaker** All together or Teams of 8 15 minutes	STEP 2: **Warm Up** Groups of 2 15 minutes	STEP 3: **Bible Study** Groups of 4 15-30 minutes	STEP 4: **Caring** Teams of 8 15-20 minutes

CROWD BREAKERS/15 Minutes

Newspaper Crumple

Here's a crowd breaker to complement this session. Divide the group into two equal teams. Fasten a rope across the room, about 4 feet off the floor. Give each team a generous stack of old newspapers.

On "go," each team must wad the newspaper and throw it over the rope to the opposing team's territory. The opposing team may then toss it back.

Call time after three or four minutes, and the team with the least amount of wadded newspaper on its side of the room is the winner. Then to start a discussion have them pick up random pieces and name the subject of the articles on that section. You can get the desired subject by putting more of a particular section in the stacks.*

Recycling Fun

The next time you collect aluminum cans for recycling, play this game before smashing the cans.

Depending on the number of cans, divide the group into teams. Each team needs 190 cans; a team may consist of one person or any number of group members. On "go," teams race to be the first to build a pyramid. Tell them to use 19 cans on the bottom row and one fewer for each new row. All the cans must be upright.

If you have only a few group members, let each person take a turn building the pyramid while being timed. The others will enjoy watching. For more fun, also race to see which team can smash and bag (or box) all its cans the quickest!

Remember to deliver the cans to a recycling center after the meeting.*

*Reprinted by permission from Group Publishing.

SESSION 4
Moral Issues

The Critics Choice

Introduction. This session is the mid-point in this course. Be sure to set aside time at the close to make a half -time report.

In this session, you will be dealing with the pressure of making moral decisions. To get started, get together with one other person in your group and make a list of the most popular programs on TV. Then, in the margin, jot down one of the following symbols to indicate the rating you would give each of these programs.

* = I enjoy this program. It is appropriate for teenagers.

P = My parents enjoy this program. The material is geared for their age.

K = If I were a parent, I would allow my kids to watch this program.

E = This program is an educational show as well as entertaining.

X = This program has too much sex and violence.

Now, start out by listing the five most popular TV programs.

TV PROGRAMS	MY RATING
_____	_____
_____	_____
_____	_____
_____	_____
_____	_____

DISCUSSION:

1. What TV program would you nominate for having the lowest moral values on TV?

2. What TV program would you nominate for having the best moral values on TV?

23

Sticking Our Neck Out

Introduction. Hollywood has made two or three films about the Bible story for this session. Try to imagine the picture of a giant banquet hall. King Herod is sitting at a drunken feast, with his brother's wife sitting next to him. Off in prison is John the Baptist, who dared to tell the King that it was wrong to sleep with his brother's wife.

Listen to the story as it develops. Then, move into groups of four and discuss the questionnaire below. Be sure to save the last 20 minutes of the session for your half-time wrap-up.

THE DEATH OF JOHN THE BAPTIST

[14]Now King Herod heard about all this, because Jesus' reputation had spread everywhere. Some people were saying, "John the Baptist has come back to life! That is why he has this power to perform miracles." . . . .

[17]Herod himself had ordered John's arrest, and he had him tied up and put in prison. Herod did this because of Herodias, whom he had married, even though she was the wife of his brother Philip, [18]John the Baptist kept telling Herod, "It isn't right for you to marry your brother's wife!"

[19]So Herodias held a grudge against John and wanted to kill him, but she could not because of Herod, [20]Herod was afraid of John because he knew that John was a good and holy man, and so he kept him safe. He liked to listen to him, even though he became greatly disturbed every time he heard him.

[21]Finally Herodias got her chance. It was on Herod's birthday, when he gave a feast for all the top government officials, the military chiefs, and the leading citizens of Galilee. [22]The daughter of Herodias came in and danced, and pleased Herod and his guests. So the king said to the girl, "What would you like to have? I will give you anything you want." [23]With many vows he said to her, "I swear that I will give you anything you ask for, even as much as half my kingdom!"

[24]So the girl went out and asked her mother, "What shall I ask for?"

"The head of John the Baptist," she answered.

[25]The girl hurried back at once to the king and demanded, "I want you to give me here and now the head of John the Baptist on a plate!"

[26]This made the king very sad, but he could not refuse her because of the vows he had made in front of all his guests. [27]So he sent off a guard at once with orders to bring John's head. The guard left, went to the prison, and cut John's head off; [28]then he brought it on a plate and gave it to the girl, who gave it to her mother. [29]When John's disciples heard about this, they came and got his body, and buried it. Mark 6:14, 17-29

Looking Into The Story: In groups of 4, let one person answer question #1, the next person question #2, etc. There are no right or wrong answers.

1. Of the four people involved in the death of John the Baptist, which one do you feel the greatest anger toward because of their moral corruption?
   a. King Herod—because he took his brother's wife and killed the person that spoke out against him
   b. Herodias—because she deserted her husband and tricked the king into killing John the Baptist
   c. Herodias' daughter—because she let her mother use her to have John the Baptist killed

2. If you could put in a good word for Herod, what would you say?
   a. he didn't want to do it
   b. he was probably drunk
   c. he kept his promise
   d. he didn't want to look bad in front of his guests

3. John the Baptist lost his head for daring to tell the king that it was wrong to take his brother's wife. Had he known of this end result, do you think he would have. . .
   a. kept his mouth shut
   b. written an anonymous "letter to the editor"
   c. said his peace and then ran for the hills
   d. done it exactly the same as he did

4. How would you describe Herodias' daughter from what you see of her in this story?
   a. a spoiled little rich girl
   b. like a lot of pretty girls—using her body to control the guys
   c. just a daughter doing what she was told
   d. blood-thirsty

My Own Story: Note the change in the sharing procedure. Go around on the first question and let everyone share their answer. Then, go around on the second question, etc.

1. Who is the John the Baptist in your school—who is willing to speak out on right and wrong, and if need be, to lose their head rather than let immorality win?
   a. our principal
   b. one of our teachers/coaches
   c. the president of our student body
   d. the captain of our football/basketball team
   e. just an ordinary guy/girl I know
   f. I don't know of anybody

2. In your family tree (including uncles, aunts, grandparents and great-grandparents) who do you admire for the way they stood up for what was right?

3. How would you rate yourself in standing up for what is right? Finish the sentence below by choosing one in each category:

IN STANDING UP FOR WHAT I THINK IS RIGHT, I AM . . .

Rock of Gibralter _____silly putty
stick to my convictions _____waver back and forth
likely to follow the crowd _____rely on my own judgment

4. When you have to make a decision, what do you do?
   a. struggle for days
   b. make a snap decision
   c. see what my friends are going to do
   d. hope it will go away
   e. take myself on a long walk
   f. ask for help

5. What is your biggest fear in standing up for what you believe?
   a. that I will be laughed at
   b. that I will be alone
   c. that I will lose my friends
   d. that I will look stupid

6. Who are the people in your life that have helped shape your moral convictions and are still on your coaching staff? Try to identify these three or four people. They can be your parents, teachers, pastors, friends.

HEAD COACH: helped you to develop your game plan and still coaches you in making decisions.

_____

ASSISTANT HEAD COACH: always there in the background, helping you to make decisions and encouraging you.

_____

TRAINER: helps out when you are injured, defeated or tuckered out. Always on call.

_____

7. If you could change your coaching staff, how would you do it? Think about these positions?

• Who's contract would you like to renew—and give them a good bonus for coaching you through the last season?

• Who would you like to add to your coaching staff?

• Who would you like to retire from the coaching staff with a wristwatch for their service to you?

Mid-Course Affirmation

Introduction. It's half time. Time for a break. Get together with your team of 8 (or the whole group if you have less than twelve) and evaluate your experience so far.

Here are two options. The second option is more risky, but a lot more personal if you have grown to appreciate each other.

Option 1: Half-time Progress Report. Turn to page three and let everyone report any growth in your life since being in this program.

Option 2: Appreciation Time. Ask one person on your team to sit in silence while the others share one thing that you have come to appreciate about this person. Finish one of these sentences:

Since being in your group, I have come to see you as. . .

   or

Since being in your group, I have come to appreciate you for your. . .

After you have gone around your group on the first person, ask the next person to sit in silence while the others finish the sentence on this person. . .etc. around the group.

This is called "strength bombardment" or "appreciation bombardment." You've done a lot of talking about yourself during this program. Now you will have a chance to hear what the others on your team have learned about you. Get set for a beautiful experience in AFFIRMATION.

If you don't know how to get started, look over the list below and pick out a word or two words that help describe what you see in this person. . .and tell them so.

I SEE YOU AS VERY. . . :

loyal	quiet	dependable	daring
fun	gorgeous	resourceful	lovable
friendly	childlike	cheerful	steady
irresistible	sensitive	meditative	spiritual
caring	unsinkable	warm	dedicated
gentle	rugged	awesome	emerging
strong	untamed	playful	crazy
courageous	special	thoughtful	energetic
encouraging	beautiful	persistent	confident

SESSION 5 - COACH'S BOX

GAME PLAN: Getting Personal. At the end of this session, the group will be introduced to a form of shared prayer—based on prayer requests. On the disclosure scale, this session will be medium to high risk.

ON THE DISCLOSURE SCALE: Session 5
No Risk_____x_____High Risk

AGENDA/FORMAT: Four parts to the meeting. Chairs are rearranged for each step in the agenda.

STEP 1:	**STEP 2:**	**STEP 3:**	**STEP 4:**
Crowd Breaker	**Warm Up**	**Bible Study**	**Caring**
All together or	Groups of 2	Groups of 4	Teams of 8
Teams of 8	15 minutes	15-30 minutes	15-20 minutes
15 minutes			

CROWD BREAKERS/15 Minutes

Magazine Scavenger Hunt

Divide into small groups and give each group several old magazines. Then, give each group a list of various items to be found in their search, such as pictures (airplane, flower, etc.) words (Coke, love, etc.) or names of famous people. When they find an item on their list, tear it out. The object is to find as many items on the list as possible in the time allowed. At the end of 10 minutes, have each group count up the number of items.

Another way to play this game is to call out a word or picture and the first group to bring this item to the center is the winner.

Dog Biscuit Relay

This hilarious relay is great for any size group.

If your group is large, divide into teams of five or more players. If your group is small, divide into two teams and repeat the relay two or more times to determine the winning team.

Have each team form a straight line with each team member down on all fours (like a dog) facing forward.

Give group members each a pinch-type clothespin to put in their mouth so the clothespin can be opened and closed with their teeth.

Put bowls with 10 to 12 dog biscuits in each on the floor in front of each team's line. The first person in each team's line must take the dog biscuits out of the bowl, one at a time, using the clothespin in his or her mouth. The biscuits are then passed on to the next person and so on down the line. If a biscuit is dropped, the person who dropped it must pick it up with the clothespin. No hands are allowed at any time.

Teams must stay in a straight line and remain on hands and knees throughout the relay.

The first team to put all its biscuits in the bowl at the end of the line wins.*

*Reprinted by permission from Group Publishing.

SESSION 5
Sexual Desires

WARM UP
Groups of 2
15 minutes

A Moment in the Sun

Introduction. This starts the second half of this program. Up to now, you have talked about the pressures in your life in general. In the second half, you will have a chance to go a little deeper and deal with some real issues.

To get started in this session, get together with one other person from your team and interview each other for a feature story on the TV program: "Lives Of The Rich and Famous."

Let your partner read the questions and you answer. Then, reverse the roles and you interview your partner.

If you have time left over, finish the two half-finished sentences at the bottom under FEEDBACK.

• What do you enjoy doing for kicks?

• What was your favorite TV show as a kid?

• Do you like going to the zoo? What fascinates you there?

• If you got into the Guinness Book of World Records, what would it be for?

• Where do you go when you want to be all alone?

• If you could marry a famous person, who would it be? Why?

• If you could live for a year anyplace in the world, where would it be?

• Do you sleep with a teddy bear?

• When was the first time you were kissed by someone outside the family?

• What is one thing you've tried that you never want to do again?

FEEDBACK: Let your partner answer these questions when you are finished with the interview.

1. What was the craziest piece of information discovered?

2. What was the most unusual thing you found out?

A Touching Incident

Introduction. In *Jesus Christ, Superstar,* a woman comes to Jesus and sings: "I Don't Know How To Love You." This story is what we are going to study in this session on sexuality.

The woman was probably a prostitute. In fact, the perfume that she poured on Jesus was probably made for her profession. Listen to the story as it unfolds. Then, move into groups of four and discuss the questionnaire. There are no right or wrong answers, so feel free to express your opinion.

Be sure to save the last 20 minutes of the session to get back together with your team.

JESUS AT THE HOME OF SIMON THE PHARISEE

36A Pharisee invited Jesus to have dinner with him, and Jesus went to his house and sat down to eat. 37In that town was a woman who lived a sinful life. She heard that Jesus was eating in the Pharisee's house, so she brought an alabaster jar full of perfume 38and stood behind Jesus, by his feet, crying and wetting his feet with her tears. Then she dried his feet with her hair, kissed them, and poured the perfume on them. 39When the Pharisee saw this, he said to himself, "If this man really were a prophet, he would know who this woman is who is touching him; he would know what kind of sinful life she lives!"

40Jesus spoke up and said to him, "Simon, I have something to tell you."

"Yes, Teacher," he said, "tell me."

41"There were two men who owed money to a moneylender," Jesus began. "One owed him five hundred silver coins, and the other owed him fifty. 42Neither of them could pay him back, so he canceled the debts of both. Which one, then, will love him more?"

43"I suppose," answered Simon, "that it would be the one who was forgiven more."

"You are right," said Jesus. 44Then he turned to the woman and said to Simon, "Do you see this woman? I came into your home, and you gave me no water for my feet, but she has washed my feet with her tears and dried them with her hair. 45You did not welcome me with a kiss, but she has not stopped kissing my feet since I came. 46You provided no olive oil for my head, but she has covered my feet with perfume. 47I tell you, then, the great love she has shown proves that her many sins have been forgiven. But whoever has been forgiven little shows only a little love."

48Then Jesus said to the woman, "Your sins are forgiven."

49The others sitting at the table began to say to themselves, "Who is this, who even forgives sins?"

50But Jesus said to the woman, "Your faith has saved you; go in peace."   Luke 7:36-50

Looking Into The Story: In groups of 4, let one person answer question #1, the next person answer question #2, etc. Remember, there are no right or wrong answers, so feel free to speak up.

1. How do you think the Pharisee knew about the reputation of the woman—that she was "sinful"?
   a. gossip
   b. she advertised
   c. he had visited her
   d. the way she dressed

2. When she entered the room and "stood behind Jesus. . .crying. . .wetting his feet with her tears. . .drying them with her hair," how did Jesus feel?
   a. embarrassed
   b. upset
   c. touched
   d. turned on
   e. wondering what she was going to do next

3. Why do you think the sinful woman expressed herself by touching Jesus instead of just saying it?
   a. because she didn't know how to express herself in words
   b. because no words could say what she felt
   c. because the Pharisee did not do these things for Jesus when Jesus arrived
   d. because she thought Jesus would appreciate it

4. Do you think there was anything sexual about the way the woman touched Jesus?
   a. no, this was just a custom that she was observing
   b. well, she may have learned some of this from her past
   c. sure, but there is a difference between normal, warm affection and sexual desire
   d. absolutely, but there is a difference between sexuality and sex

5. Why did Jesus let the woman touch him like he did if he knew she was a sinful woman?
   a. he wanted to affirm her sexuality but let her know that what she had done with her sexuality was wrong
   b. he wanted to teach the Pharisee that there was a difference between sexuality and sex
   c. he wanted to allow the woman to express her feelings for him in a non-sexual way
   d. everyone needs to be touched, even Jesus

My Own Story: Note the different approaches to sharing. Go around on question #1 and let everyone explain their answer. Then, go around again on question #2, etc.

1. Do you think that Jesus had the same sexual desires that you have?
   a. I hope not
   b. well, if he was human, he must have had the same desires
   c. evidently—he talked about it a lot
   d. I never thought about it before

2. How do you feel about the sexual desires you have?
   a. they make me frustrated and irritable
   b. I feel guilty because Christians shouldn't have these feelings
   c. they make life exciting
   d. they are natural and I accept them
   e. I am struggling with how to handle them in a Christian way

3. Which of these phrases reflect your view of sexuality?
   a. sexuality is an important part of being human
   b. sexuality is feeling good about being a boy/girl
   c. sexuality brings too much pressure to life
   d. sexuality is overly identified with sexual activity
   e. sexuality is overemphasized in our society
   f. you can express your sexuality without being sexually active

4. Who is the person you admire and is a role model for you for a healthy view of sex and sexuality?
   a. my mother/father
   b. a close relative
   c. an athlete by the name of_____
   d. a movie star/famous person by the name of_____
   e. my teacher/coach
   f. my pastor/priest/youth leader
   g. frankly, I don't have a role model

5. If you had been in Jesus' shoes when this very sensual woman came in and started touching you, what would you have done?
   a. I would feel awfully funny
   b. I would get turned on
   c. I would be afraid she was trying to get to me
   d. I would have recognized that she was not trying to get to me
   e. I'm not sure, touching someone like this usually leads to something more
   f. I would get out of there—fast!

6. Which of the following expresses your own attitude toward touching and being touched?
   a. I want and need to be touched and hugged more
   b. I'm suspicious of people who want to touch me
   c. I want to be touched and hugged, but worry if it's OK
   d. people should avoid touching and hugging—it brings too much temptation
   e. to be close emotionally, you have to be able to touch physically

Getting Personal

Introduction. Here are two options to close the session on problems.

Option 1: Follow the usual procedure. Regather as teams and report-in on the session—what you learned—and spend some time in prayer with your prayer partner.

Option 2: Try a new form of sharing prayer requests and praying for one another. If you choose this option, here are the instructions.

1. Get together in groups of three.

2. Let one person share a prayer request by answering the question:

How can we help you in prayer this week?

3. The other two in the three-some respond to this prayer request in this way:

• One person prays a prayer of THANKS. . .

"God, I want to THANK YOU for (name). . . ."

• The other person prays a prayer of PETITION. . .

"God, I ask your help for my friend (name), for. . . ."

4. When you have finished with the first person, let the next person share a request and the other two pray for this person, etc. . . around the group of three.

Remember, in your group of three, you start out by letting one person answer this question:

How can we help you in prayer this week?

SESSION 6 - COACH'S BOX

GAME PLAN: Learning to Care. At the end of this session, the group members will be invited to share their needs and to reach out and care for one another. On the disclosure scale, this session will be high risk.

ON THE DISCLOSURE SCALE: Session 6.
No Risk_____x___High Risk

AGENDA/FORMAT: Four parts to the meeting. Chairs are rearranged for each step in the agenda.

STEP 1: **Crowd Breaker** All together or Teams of 8 15 minutes	STEP 2: **Warm Up** Groups of 2 15 minutes	STEP 3: **Bible Study** Groups of 4 15-30 minutes	STEP 4: **Caring** Teams of 8 15-20 minutes

CROWD BREAKERS/15 Minutes

Disney Character Name Guess

Make individual name tags with the many Disney characters. Pin a name on the back of each person. They are then to guess the name by asking only one question of a person (who also gets to ask only one question of them). After the exchange of one question, each individual then goes to another person in the room and proceeds to ask another question to discover their Disney character.

This is great fun and informal interaction. Some suggested characters are: Dumbo, Tigger, Bambi, Lady, Peter Pan, Pluto, Jiminy Cricket, Anastasia, Goofy, Captain Hook, Love Bug, Sleeping Beauty, Pete's Dragon (Eliot), Piglet, Christopher Robin, Happy, Prince Charming, Doc, Flower, Thumper, Pinocchio, Winnie the Pooh, Donald Duck, Snow White, Eeyore, Fairy Godmother, Cinderella.

It's the Pits

It's the Pits is a whole evening of activities.

Start the evening with Pit Pass. Divide the group into equal teams (six to ten on a team). Give each team a Nerf ball. On "go," each member of the team passes the ball from armpit to armpit without the assistance of hands. If the ball is dropped or touched by a team member's hand, the team starts over again. The first team to pass the ball successfully to each member and then back is the winner.

Pit Food is next on the list of activities. Gather as many different types of pitted foods as you can find—cherries, plums, peaches, prunes, olives and apricots. This race shows who can eat the fastest. Between each eating event, the eater sends a runner to the closest restroom (for a pit stop) to bring back one square of toilet paper in which to place the pits.

*Reprinted by permission from Group Publishing.

SESSION 6
Spiritual Struggles

Redecorating My Room/Life

Introduction. If you could redecorate your room with the posters listed below, what would you choose for these crucial spots in your bedroom?

- A poster over your desk—where you study
- A poster next to your mirror—where you look at yourself
- A poster on the outside of your door—for others to see
- A poster behind the door—that only you can see when the door is closed

Jot down these key words next to the posters you select: (1) desk, (2) mirror, (3) outside the door, and (4) behind the door.

_____	Quiet! Genius at work
_____	Lord, make me an instrument of your peace
_____	I finally got it together—but I forgot where I put it
_____	Don't bug me. I'm pedaling as fast as I can
_____	Bloom where you are planted
_____	Today is the first day of the rest of your life
_____	Soccer players need love, too
_____	Fragile! Handle with care
_____	When life hands you a lemon, make lemonade
_____	You will find happiness in the ones you love
_____	I don't need a great deal of love but I need a steady supply
_____	I can do all things through Christ who strengthens me
_____	Prayer changes things.
_____	Expect a miracle
_____	I believe in the sun, even if it does not shine
_____	Keep your mind with all diligence, for out of it are the issues of life
_____	There is no medicine stronger than love
_____	Something good is going to happen to you
_____	The power of God is at work here

Finding Christ on Your Road

Introduction. Hassles with God may not belong in this course on pressure, but we are going to study this anyway because your relationship with God influences everything else in your life.

The Bible story you will look at is a familiar one—the conversion of Paul. The Apostle Paul grew up as a very religious person. In fact, in his early life, he led the persecution of Christians and was responsible for stoning a Christian by the name of Stephen. But God "hassled" this guy to the ground and turned him around.

Listen to the story. Then, move into groups of four and discuss the questionnaire: (1) **Looking Into The Story**—about the Bible story, and (2) **My Own Story**—about your own experience.

Save the last 15-20 minutes in the session for the Caring time.

THE CONVERSION OF SAUL

¹In the meantime Saul kept up his violent threats of murder against the followers of the Lord. He went to the High Priest ²and asked for letters of introduction to the synagogues in Damascus, so that if he should find there any followers of the Way of the Lord, he would be able to arrest them, both men and women, and bring them back to Jerusalem.

³As Saul was coming near the city of Damascus, suddenly a light from the sky flashed around him. ⁴He fell to the ground and heard a voice saying to him, "Saul, Saul! Why do you persecute me?"

⁵"Who are you, Lord?" he asked.

"I am Jesus, whom you persecute," the voice said. ⁶"But get up and go into the city, where you will be told what you must do."

⁷The men who were traveling with Saul had stopped, not saying a word; they heard the voice but could not see anyone. ⁸Saul got up from the ground and opened his eyes, but could not see a thing. So they took him by the hand and led him into Damascus. ⁹For three days he was not able to see, and during that time he did not eat or drink anything.

¹⁰There was a believer in Damascus named Ananias. He had a vision, in which the Lord said to him, "Ananias!"

"Here I am, Lord," he answered.

¹¹The Lord said to him, "Get ready and go to Straight Street, and at the house of Judas ask for a man from Tarsus named Saul. He is praying, ¹²and in a vision he has seen a man named Ananias come in and place his hands on him so that he might see again." . . .

¹⁷So Ananias went, entered the house where Saul was, and placed his hands on him. "Brother Saul," he said, "the Lord has sent me—Jesus himself, who appeared to you on the road as you were coming here. He sent me so that you might see again and be filled with the Holy Spirit." ¹⁸At once something like fish scales fell from Saul's eyes, and he was able to see again. He stood up and was baptized; ¹⁹and after he had eaten, his strength came back.

Acts 9:1-12.17-19

Looking Into The Story: In groups of 4, let one person answer question #1, the next person answer question #2, etc. around the group. Remember, there are no right or wrong answers, so feel free to speak up.

1. If Paul went to your school, what would he be?
   a. serious-minded student
   b. captain of the wrestling team
   c. drop out—one of the motorcycle gang
   d. president of the Bible club
   e. debate team—national champion
   f. party kid
   g. bully
   h. fighter for student rights

2. Why do you think he wanted to go to Damascus (300 miles from Jerusalem) and arrest some more Christians?
   a. he hated God
   b. he wanted to please God
   c. he belonged to a cult
   d. he was a bully
   e. he believed in ethnic cleansing

3. How do you think Paul felt in the three days that he sat in his room in Damascus—blind—trying to figure out what happened to him?
   a. wiped out
   b. confused
   c. scared to death
   d. angry
   e. wondering

4. How would you describe what happened to Paul on the road to Damascus to the kids in your school with no religious background?
   a. God zapped him
   b. God and Paul had a little confrontation
   c. God took Paul behind the gym and beat the tar out of him
   d. Paul got blind-sided by God
   e. I don't think the kids in my school would understand

5. What impact did this experience have upon the rest of Paul's life?
   a. not a whole lot
   b. it shook him up a little
   c. it completely changed the direction of his life
   d. it caused him to change churches but that's all

6. How do you think Ananias felt when God told him to go to Saul and lay hands on him?
   a. scared to death
   b. surprised
   c. thrilled
   d. wondering—you must be kidding

My Own Story: Note the change in sharing procedure. Go around your group on question #1, and let everyone share their answer. Then, go around again on question #2, etc. through the questions.

1. Where have you found Christ along the road of your life?
   a. when the road has been rough and I needed help to keep going
   b. when the road has been easy, I've coasted, and was thankful
   c. when I was angry like Paul, and not looking for him, he showed up
   d. he's been there every step of the way
   e. I don't know, but I think I see him up ahead
   f. he must be on some other road, because I haven't seen him

2. If you could compare your spiritual journey to Paul's experience, where are you right now?
   a. on the road to Damascus
   b. starting to hear God call out my name and wondering what God is trying to tell me
   c. experiencing some of the same emotions that Paul went through
   d. starting to sort out what has been happening

3. Ananias was sent by God to come alongside of Paul in his crisis. Who has come alongside of you to help you sort out what is going on?
   a. my parent
   b. my youth leader/pastor
   c. one or two friends
   d. my brother/sister
   e. no one

4. If Paul had been brought to your youth group and explained what happened to him, how would your youth group receive his story?
   a. we would laugh him out of the room
   b. we would listen politely and consider him a little weird
   c. we would want to make him feel accepted
   d. we would welcome him into our group and share some of our own experiences with God
   e. other:_____

5. If you had to explain to little children how God breaks into your life, how would you describe it?
   a. it is like getting to know a friend
   b. it is like waking up one morning and you are a different person
   c. it is like coming into the world as a baby
   d. it is like a bolt of lightning
   e. it is like getting a puppy for your birthday
   f. it is like_____

Learning to Care

Introduction: You are nearly through with this course as a youth group. Next week, you will have a chance to celebrate and decide what you are going to do next.

To prepare for your last session together, take a few minutes right now and reflect on what and where you have changed during this course. If you have stayed with the same team throughout this course, you will be able to say how you have seen your teammates change. If you don't know each other that well, you will do the talking for yourself. Here are two steps to follow.

1. **Affirmation.** Go around and let everyone on your team answer one or more of the questions below. Again, if you know each other, use this opportunity to share how you have seen your teammates grow.

   • Where have you grown in your own life during this course?
   • Where have you seen growth in some of the others in your group during this course?
   • What have you appreciated most about the group during this course?

2. **Option.** At this point, your team can choose one of two ways to close the meeting.

   • **Option 1: Prayer Partners.** Get together with your prayer partner and report on your week. Then close in prayer.

   • **Option 2: Circle of Love.** Stay together with your team and express your feelings for each other non-verbally. Here is how. Follow carefully:

   a. Stand in a circle—about a foot apart
   b. Everyone puts their right hand in front of them—palm up
   c. Team leader steps into the circle and goes to one person. Looks them in the eyes for a few seconds. Then, takes their hand and tries to express the care you feel for this person by doing something to their hand—such as gripping it firmly, stroking it, shaking it. . .etc. Use only appropriate gestures.
   d. After the Team Leader has gone around the circle, the next person goes around the circle in the same way, etc. . . until everyone has gone around the circle.

   Remember, all of this is done without words.

   BUT IN SHAKING THE HANDS OF THOSE IN YOUR GROUP, YOU CAN SAY A LOT—HOW YOU CARE!

SESSION 7 - COACH'S BOX

GAME PLAN: Team Celebration. At the close of this session, you can have a special worship service (see below) or a party to evaluate and celebrate your experience as a team. On the disclosure scale, this session will be no risk to high risk, depending on what you choose.

ON THE DISCLOSURE SCALE: Session 7
No Risk_x_____x_High Risk

AGENDA/FORMAT: Four parts to the meeting. Chairs are rearranged for each step in the agenda.

STEP 1:	STEP 2:	STEP 3:	STEP 4:
Crowd Breaker	**Warm Up**	**Bible Study**	**Caring**
All together or	Groups of 2	Groups of 4	Teams of 8
Teams of 8	15 minutes	15-30 minutes	15-20 minutes
15 minutes			

CROWD BREAKER/15 Minutes

Putting on the Gospel Hits

This idea uses contemporary Christian music for a lip-sync contest. Plan a special contest night and invite church members and friends. Select a few judges and score each contestant or air band. Use this point system:

Area	Top Score
Originality	30 points
Appearance	30 points
Lip-sync	30 points

Give Christian concert tickets or a popular Christian album as an award for the best act (whoever scores the most points). Let young people briefly tell about the song they chose to perform. Have them stress the importance of the words or message it portrays.*

SERENDIPITY SERVICE/30 minutes. A Caring time closing exercise for the whole youth group. If you choose to use this activity, allow enough time. You may have to shorten other parts of the meeting.

Use a quiet meditative place for this time where students can worship and share how God has worked in their lives in the past weeks. A prayer room, fireside, candlelight in your regular room, etc. will help make this a unique experience. Introduce a period of sharing by leading the group in some worship songs and then have each of them explain what God is asking them to do or the next move in their lives in light of what they have learned and experienced. Then have that person kneel or sit in the center of the group while the others reach in to touch and pray for this person to do as God is leading them. Let one person voice the prayer for the whole group. Continue until each person has shared and been commissioned to move forward with God.

*Reprinted by permission from Group Publishing.

SESSION 7
Decisions, Decisions

Crystal Ball

Introduction. Instead of the usual Warm Up exercise, we want you to use this time to get ready for the Wrap Up exercise at the close of this session. At that time, you will regather as a team (the same people you have been with during this course) and have a chance to share your insights about one another. Below are a list of predictions about the people on your team—like they do for graduating seniors in the high school yearbook. In silence, jot down the names of the people in your group next to the thing you feel they might accomplish in the next few years.

Do NOT tell anyone what you have thought about giving each person. This will happen at the closing celebration. You have 5 minutes for this exercise.

THE PERSON IN OUR GROUP MOST LIKELY TO. . .

_____ take Joe Montana's place in the Hall of Fame

_____ become a movie star like_____

_____ skateboard across the country

_____ open a charm school for Hell's Angels

_____ become a famous model for Parisian negligees

_____ run a dating bureau for middle aged bachelors

_____ rise to the top in the Mafia

_____ be the first woman to win the Indianapolis 500

_____ get busted for skinnydipping in the public park

_____ win the lottery and retire to the South Sea Islands

_____ join the French Foreign Legion

_____ make a fortune on pay toilet rentals

_____ be the sales woman of the year for aerobic gear

_____ write a best selling novel based on all the dates they had

_____ set a world record for blowing bubble gum

_____ get listed in the *Guinness Book of World Records* for the messiest car

Excuses, Excuses!

Introduction. The Bible study for this session has been deliberately chosen for this last session in the course on pressure.

In this course, you have looked at pressure from stress, from parental expectations, from peers, from moral issues, from sexual desires and from spiritual struggles. In each case, you have been asked to do something about your life or lifestyle. In this session, you are going to be making some decisions about the future—about the future of your life and about the future of your youth group.

In the Bible study, you will meet three guys who made excuses about spiritual things because they were busy. In the process, you will have a chance to look at your own priorities and see if you have your own priorities in order. You need to plan now to devote the better part of the time in this session to the decision-making time at the close.

Now move into groups of four and listen to the Bible story. Then, discuss the questionnaire.

THE PARABLE OF THE GREAT FEAST

[15] When one of the guests sitting at the table heard this, he said to Jesus, "How happy are those who will sit down at the feast in the Kingdom of God?"

[16] Jesus said to him, "There was once a man who was giving a great feast to which he invited many people. [17] When it was time for the feast, he sent his servant to tell his guests, 'Come, everything is ready!' [18] But they all began, one after another, to make excuses. The first one told the servant, 'I have bought a field and must go and look at it; please accept my apologies.' [19] Another one said, 'I have bought five pairs of oxen and am on my way to try them out; please accept my apologies.' [20] Another one said, 'I have just gotten married, and for that reason I cannot come.' [21] The servant went back and told all this to his master. The master was furious and said to his servant, 'Hurry out to the streets and alleys of the town, and bring back the poor, the crippled, the blind, and the lame.' [22] Soon the servant said, 'Your order has been carried out, sir, but there is room for more.' [23] So the master said to the servant, 'Go out to the country roads and lanes and make people come in, so that my house will be full. [24] I tell you all that none of those who were invited will taste my dinner!'"

Luke 14:15-24

Looking Into The Story: In groups of 4, let one person answer question #1, the next person answer question #2, etc. around the group.

1. If you had been the person that prepared the great feast, how would you have felt when the guests you invited all made excuses?
   a. disappointed/hurt   d. I would be crushed
   b. angry   e. I would brush it off
   c. I'd never talk to them again

2. Which excuse would you consider legitimate? If you had to excuse one of these guys, who would it be?
a. the guy who had just bought a farm and wanted to inspect it
b. the guy who had just bought a tractor (oxen) and wanted to try it out
c. the guy who just got married

3. Why do you think these guys made excuses?
a. they were not party people
b. they were really busy
c. they thought they had better things to do
d. they didn't like the person who was throwing the party
e. they didn't know how good the party was going to be

4. When the special guests refused, who did the master invite to the feast?
a. the red-neck kids at school
b. the kids from across town
c. the losers
d. the party crowd
e. the kids who are open to spiritual things

My Own Story: Note the change in sharing procedure. Go around on question #1 and let everyone answer. Then, go around on question #2, etc.

1. If God called you on the phone today and invited you to a special feast he was giving, what would you do?
a. figure my friends were making crank calls again
b. ask the person what he was selling
c. check it out
d. jump at the chance

2. How would you describe your spiritual diet lately?
a. baby food
b. TV dinners
c. junk food
d. fast food
e. church picnic
f. chicken every Sunday
g. full-course banquet

3. What would it take to get you to come to God's banquet of spiritual nourishment?
a. a few friends to join me
b. lively entertainment and fun
c. an adjustment in my priorities
d. more hunger than I have at the moment
e. just a little encouragement

4. During this course, where have you made the most progress in your spiritual life?
   a. personal discipline
   b. moral development
   c. spiritual development
   d. mental attitude
   e. self-acceptance
   f. Bible understanding
   g. willingness to open up and share
   h. concern for others
   i. attitude about school
   j. family relationships

5. What is the next big challenge you need to face?
   a. settling down
   b. learning how to focus my energy
   c. making moral decisions
   d. relationships with the opposite sex
   e. developing my self-confidence
   f. finding some friends who will help me
   g. dealing with my relationship at home
   h. building a deeper relationship with God

CARING
Teams of 8
15-20 minutes

What Happened?

Introduction: You have two options for this special closing experience: (1) The worship service described in the Coach's Box, or (2) A de-briefing session, using the agenda below.

1. Warm Up Exercise: Regather as teams (or the entire youth group together) and share the results of the Warm Up exercise. Ask one person to sit in silence while everyone on their team explains where they have put this person's name and why. Then, move to the next person, etc. around the group. Use this opportunity to share your appreciation for the contributions you have made to each other in the team.

2. Evaluation: Go around on the first question below and let everyone explain their answer. Then, go around again on the next question, etc.

   A. When you first started on this course, what did you think about it?
      a. I liked it
      b. I had some reservations
      c. I only came for the fun
      d. I was bored
      e. other:_____

B. How would you describe the experience of opening up and sharing your ideas and problems with this group?

a. scary
b. very difficult
c. exciting
d. a life-changing experience

e. invaluable
f. okay, but. . .
g. just what I needed
h. a beautiful breakthrough

C. What was the high point in this program for you?

a. fun
b. times of prayer
c. feeling of belonging to others who really care
d. being with teammates who are committed to Christ
e. knowing I am not alone in my problems
f. finding myself again
g. Bible study
h. learning to deal with my hang-ups

3. Personal Change. Turn back to page 3 and let everyone explain where they have changed during this course.

4. What's Next. As a group, decide what you are going to do next.

A Word To The Youth Leaders

Congratulations. You are working with the most potential-packed audience in the world—Teenagers. This is one of the most difficult times in their lives. They are making big decisions, often alone or in packs. Peers are important to them and there is tremendous pressure to do what peers demand and the chance to think critically about choices. This youth program is designed to give teenagers a feeling of belonging. A family of peers. An alternative to the gang at school. Or an alternative inside of the school.

This program is built around the idea of teamwork. The goal is to help youth "bring out the best in one another." By agreeing on a set of goals. Agreeing on a level of commitment for a period of time (seven weeks). By setting ground rules, and holding each other accountable. If this sounds like something out of educational psychology, it is. The dynamics are the same. The only difference is the motive and the learning objective. The goal of this program is spiritual formation. Christian orientation. Christian value clarification. Christian moral development. Christian commitment.

The Importance Of Voluntary Commitment

The difference between this program and the typical youth program in the church is the commitment level. To get into this program, a youth *must* commit himself or herself to being in the program. This means "choosing" to be in the program every session for seven weeks, to be a team player in order to make the group process work.

Anyone who has been involved in team sports will understand this principle. And anyone who has coached a team will understand the role of the student pastor or youth leader. The youth leader is the coach and the youth group is the squad. And the squad is broken up into small units or teams of six to eight—with a sub-coach or facilitator inside of each team.

Structure Of The Youth Meetings

The meetings look like typical training workouts of a sports camp. First, the whole squad meets together for some limbering up exercises (all together or by teams of eight competing against one another if you have a large youth group). Then, the entire squad pairs off for some basic, one-on-one "conversation starters" to break the ice. Then, with your partner, groups of four are formed for the Bible Study discussion. Finally, the team of eight is regathered for a little wrap-up and caring for each other. The typical meeting looks like this:

Step 1: Crowd Breaker Team of 8 or all together	Step 2: Conversation Starters/ Groups of 2	Step 3: Bible Study/ Groups of 4 or half of team	Step 4: Wrap Up and Caring/ Teams of 8

Moving from the large group (Step 1) to groups of two (Step 2) to groups of 4 (Step 3) to groups of 8 (Step 4) will not only offer a spontaneity to the meeting, but will also position the youth to be in the best size of group for the particular type of activity.

Step 1:	Step 2:	Step 3:	Step 4:
Purpose: To Kick off the meeting.	Purpose: To start a relationship	Purpose: To discuss Bible Story	Purpose: To care for one another.

 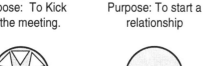

In the first session in this course, the ideal would be to form teams of eight that can stay together for the entire course. This could be done by random selection or by designating the teams to break up cliques. Or it can be done in a serendipitous fashion by giving out slips of song titles and having the youth find out who is on their team by whistling their song until they "find each other." For junior highs, we recommend that an adult or older youth be in each team of eight.

If you only have fifteen or twenty youth in your entire group, you could keep all of the squad together for Step 1 and Step 4, and break into 2's and 4's for Step 2 and Step 3.

In Case of Emergency, Read the Instructions

In the margin beside each Step, you will find instructions to the leader. Read this. Sometimes, the instructions are important. Trust us. We have written this program based on our experience. Give the program a chance. There is method to the madness. Particularly, the fast-paced movement from 2's to 4's to 8's.

Get a commitment out of your youth before you start the program for seven weeks or seven sessions. And remind them (by thanking them every week) for making this commitment. Here's to the thing that God is about to do in your youth. Here's to the future of your church—your youth.

Serendipity House is a publisher specializing in small groups. Serendipity has been providing training and resources for youth ministry for over 30 years. As we continue to develop materials for youth groups, we would love to hear your comments, ideas or suggestions. Call us at 1-800-525-9563.

The Serendipity Youth Bible Study Series is the culmination of forty years in youth ministry for Lyman Coleman, the author of the series.

Lyman Coleman started out in youth work in the 50's with Young Life while he was a student at Baylor University in Texas, and with the Navigators while doing graduate work at Biblical Seminary in New York and New York University.

In the 60's, he pioneered a variety of team-building programs for youth that combined group work with outreach missions: the coffee house (*The Coffee House Itch*), folk musicals (*Man Alive*), film making (*Festival*), and multi-media happenings *(Kaleidoscope).*

In the 70's, he integrated the strategies of values clarification, moral development and interactive Bible study in a series of youth courses for Word Books, entitled *The Serendipity Youth Series.* He also created the special huddle programs for the Fellowship of Christian Athletes and parent courses for World Wide Marriage Encounter (*Evenings for Couples* and *Evenings for Parents).*

In the 80's, he collaborated with Denny Rydberg (President of Young Life) in a series of youth Bible study courses covering the felt needs of youth. He also was the general editor of the *Serendipity Bible for Groups.*

In the 90's he designed the scope and sequence library of resources for spiritual formation in the church through elective support groups covering all levels of spiritual formation—in which the *Youth Bible Study Series* is a part.

Hundreds of youth workers have contributed their ideas and dozens of youth leaders have had a part in the writing in the formative years, especially David Stone, Don Kimball, Dr. Richard Peace, Denny Rydberg, Keith Madsen and the Serendipity Staff.

Lyman lives in Littleton, Colorado, with his wife, Margaret, and three grown children and their families.

SERENDIPITY HOUSE is a publishing house that creates programs like this one for many types of groups in the church: kick off groups, Bible study groups, support groups, recovery groups and mission/task groups. The philosophy behind these groups is the same: (1) help the group agree upon their purpose and ground rules, (2) spend the first few sessions you are together getting acquainted, (3) shift gears in Bible study as the group matures, and (4) help the group say "goodbye" and decompress when they are through with their purpose.